Sonnets of Innocence and Experience

William Peskett

A Cycad Books Production
Pattaya, Thailand
Also published as an e-book
Cover: Dodos in the Natural History Museum, London

E X L I B R I S   8 5 7 2 9 4 7 7 0 2

ISBN: 9798634786285

Nought loves another as itself

Nor venerates another so.

Nor is it possible to Thought

A greater than itself to know:

WILLIAM BLAKE (1757-1827)
A Little Boy Lost
From *Songs of Experience* (1794)

Contents

Innocence

There was a time of knowing less than now
But understanding more; that dream has gone.
Unseen, we let it slip away somehow.
What's left that we can base our lives upon?
Respecting nature, we survived those days
As thoughtful hunters on the open veldt,
Developing the skills that nowadays
Consultants and accountants are not dealt.
We had a sacred contract with the land,
A deal for the survival of the fit;
Our epic journeys, risky and unplanned,
Procured new pastures we would never quit.
From understanding all we struggled hence
Then lost it lusting for experience.

Tattoo

Though there are works of art I rave about –
The fighting ship and Bosch's view of sin;
That statue Michelangelo chipped out –
I'd never have them inked beneath my skin.
Life's beauty was conceived before we came,
Its symmetry and schemes to keep from harm.
Our efforts to enhance it just seem lame –
A crown and anchor needled on an arm.
While Maori chiefs must demonstrate their power
And jolly tars will while the hours at sea,
A woman's breast embellished with a flower
Diminishes her charm, at least to me.
The world's so full of tat, too late for you
To buck the trend, so you get tattooed too.

Retinal

Now from the mirror two eyes look at me
And one looks back; the other one is blind.
My retina's not where it's meant to be;
It's come adrift and water's seeped behind.
The surgeon sucks the jelly from my eye,
Replacing it by pumping propane in.
The retina is squeezed until it's dry,
Like blowing on a bowl of custard skin.
The trouble was my eye was full of haze,
Restricting me to half my usual view.
The bubble should be gone in fourteen days,
Restoring my abilities anew.
This scare has made me grateful to be whole
By shuttering a window to my soul.

Kiss

Who's certain when a kiss becomes a kiss?
While one mouth reaches up the other dips
And all the space between is certain bliss,
The sense that lips have of approaching lips.
The eyes are certain of the mouth's approach;
The movement's slow, it moves at measured pace.
The lips part slowly, wary to encroach
On what lies hidden in the trembling space.
Unwary eyes, to like eyes, now reveal –
Which once with other lovers hid too much –
The time is right for trembling lips to feel
The disappearing space as lovers touch.
When all the space between is certain bliss,
Who's certain when a kiss becomes a kiss?

To burp is human; to belch, bovine

To dairy cows the news comes with a thud,
Providing them with much to ruminate:
For ages they have blithely chewed the cud,
Yet now we lay our problems at their gate.
While human halitosis can spell death
To moments of romance when love is near,
At least when we exhale our torrid breath
It doesn't kill the actual atmosphere.
Across our verdant meadows cows may range,
Dispensing methane as they puff and wheeze,
Yet we can't sense the climate or its change
In air-conned delis where we buy our cheese.
Now beef and dairy, staples in the past,
Indulged by hordes of humans cannot last.

Asian Tsunami 15 years on

Tsunamis happen centuries apart,
Too long for any memory to survive
Of how the sea retreats before they start –
So fast that fish are picked up still alive.
If memories then could offer us no aid,
Today we're surely better placed to warn,
To notify the errors that we made
To our descendants who are not yet born.
But have we learned the lessons of the past?
Are plans in place to show them where to go?
Or when they see the ocean sinking fast
Will they, as we did, stop to watch the show?
The horn of the loudspeaker's blocked by vines;
And rust grows on the muster-station signs.

First love

I took you walking and you took my hand.
Then, showing me not everyone's the same,
You kindled fires I didn't understand;
I couldn't breathe and not incant your name.
Though fifty years are gone, I still have you;
Your scent is on my fingers to this day.
Though senseless now in all I used to do,
I'd find you blindfold in a grove of may.
The courses of our lives are fixed by whim;
Those junctions on the highway are mundane.
My urge to travel now is growing dim –
Avoid the passion and you miss the pain.
Now take my heart, I'm handing you the knife;
I've loved you every decade of my life.

Quantum theory

We wake, we sleep; our lives play out in lots,
The days bleep by like photons one by one;
The brightness splits into a stream of dots,
The darkness quiet between when day is done.
Each episode's a chance for routine thought,
For recollection and a plan to act.
Have we achieved the things we think we ought
Or put them off in some affected pact?
A lifetime's made of atoms, that is all,
Like blood cells jostling down a pulsing pipe.
These satisfactions, added, should enthral;
Reality is of a different stripe.
We're born, we live, we start our slow decline;
We come, we go, our dots become a line.

Jean Agélou, photographer

Please hold that pose a moment more, Fernande,
And lift your line of vision up to me.
'No nudity,' that smirking gendarme warned,
Then lurked about to see what he might see.
What he does not appreciate, that runt,
With his grotesque concern for pubic hair,
Is how my snaps are valued at the front.
Without you, love, we'll never win *la Guerre*.
Now smile a little and reveal a breast,
Then part your lips and let them hear you croon;
To see you is to know you; you're their best –
You give them hope their hell will finish soon.
It's for our lads who wade through stink and mud
And grip you as they fall, all flecked with blood.

First

Of all our generations one was first
To knap a stone and hurl a pointed spear,
To mix up paint, become the first to hear
Another's thoughts and have their own reversed.
Now different from their parents, in their arms
Their babies' lives would differ yet again.
Then their descendants would swap seeds for grain
And harness beasts of burden on their farms.
For these pioneers the past did not exist –
Survive the present was the task at hand,
Exploit all living things and quell the land;
The sunlit future still was veiled in mist.
To start our journey they did not intend;
They couldn't know the way, nor see the end.

Meat and two veg

Intelligent design is meant to be
The means by which a supernatural hand
Guides evolution to the life we see –
So everything is purposeful and planned.
This may explain the beauty of an eye
And how a nest is organised by ants,
But rather leaves us stranded high and dry
Explaining what a man keeps in his pants.
As men sought game to griddle on the fire –
Before they even thought of wearing threads –
They must have stridden through both thorn and briar
And ripped their soft and dangly parts to shreds.
If this is right, men now know who to blame:
That smart designer, smiling, is a dame.

Tree

Just as a delta splits its mother flow
To rivulets so fine they're lost in sand,
Your mighty trunk divides both high and low
To bond the elements of air and land.
In soil your tendrils seek out specks of grit
And prise their molecules of water loose;
They hold on fast, determined not to quit
When thunderous winds unleash their wild abuse.
On every twig your leaves seek out the sun
And craft comestibles from thinnest air.
Your pores close over when the day is done,
When moisture from the earth, though sweet, is rare.
Our foul pollution you refine to wood.
Where all our works are bad, you make them good.

Whisky

When Marlowe says that he could use a drink,
The blonde pours him a whisky, and it's neat,
For dames in movies do not tend to think
That gin could be a real man's cup of meat.
Those wild-west farm hands, dusty from the range
Are apt to ask for red-eye when they dine.
It's what men do – besides, it would look strange
To be a tough guy with a dry white wine.
Now gumshoes, cowboys, plus more types like that:
To call them good role models would be risky.
But admiration makes me raise my hat
To those whose choice inebriant is whisky.
So if your grog's your mistress and your wife,
Let's not drink water, but water of life.

There and then

To live with nature doesn't always mean
That dwelling in a glade is free from strife;
Our values sorely lacking, we demean
The meagre value of a human life.
With tools, our violence took a tragic turn,
Much deadlier than brawling in the mud.
In innocence, it serves our needs to burn
Our vanquished foes and wield our power with blood.
The ruthless are respected, killers brave,
Infanticide and rape don't raise our scorn;
A soldier lost in war becomes a slave,
The poor are poor if that's the way they're born.
Our learning brings no favour, never can,
Till, willingly, we prize our fellow man.

Lamb

There are no wild ones who can set you free,
No feral mutton that can hear your bleat.
You're fastened to the pasture and must see
Your sibling flock in terms of wool and meat.
The farmer made you, unsuspecting lamb,
From scrawny stock that ranged the mountain rocks
To make a pleasant change from common ham
And turn your winter coat to woollen socks.
The farmer made you, yet you've everything:
You're given land, you're fed and kept from harm.
Your farmer is your midwife in the spring;
Like you, he is a prisoner of the farm.
To live a life of plenty with her ram,
What ewe would not give up her fleece, her lamb?

Hospital

In here you're changed to infantile or old;
The simplest tasks are done on your behalf.
You quickly learn to do as you are told
And not attempt to second-guess the staff.
No matter that your legs are strong and fit,
Your journey down the hall is in a chair,
And if you have the nerve to question it,
You learn each pill is vital for your care.
Quips may relieve the stresses you endure
But doctors have no time for puerile jokes;
You're just a body looking for a cure –
Their favourites are the ones struck dumb by strokes.
In bed, attention rains down from above;
For you, but not for them, it feels like love.

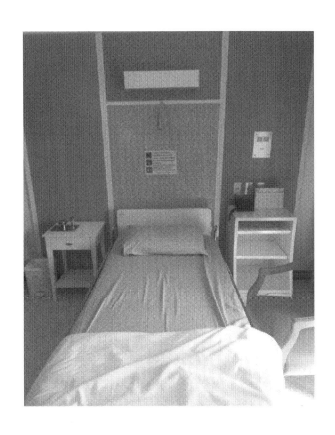

Last love

Our love's a gem but time's a feline thief
And my libido wears an evening gown.
As evidently life is all too brief
We must make hay before the sun goes down.
The list begins with learning how to live
When one of us (that's you) is left alone.
But time spent teaching all I have to give
Is time not lived, so in effect is blown.
A jungle girl, you knew which fruits were safe
And, someway, how to be a city wife.
Eliza of the tropics, queen from waif,
You found me on my own and saved my life.
Let's not dispute who first will be bereft,
But love our time; it's all the time that's left.

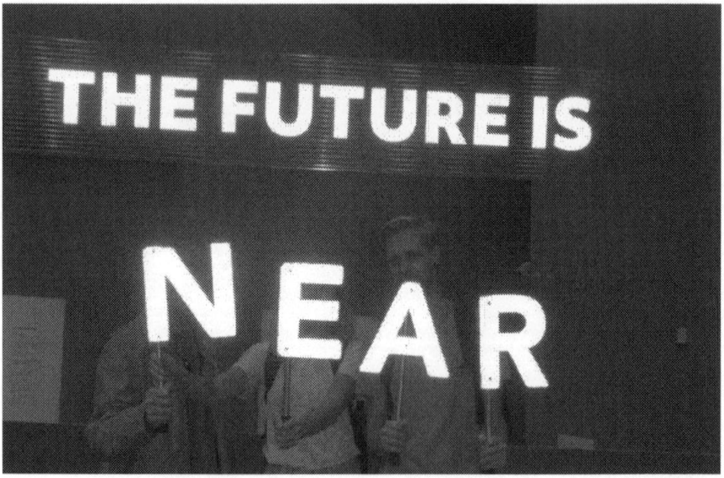
THE FUTURE IS
NEAR

Experience

Our memory is vast but we forget,
We have the biggest brain but do not think,
We boast that we alone have reason, yet
We push our own survival to the brink.
The way we live our lives has changed so fast;
The trick was not to take each step anew,
But build each iteration on the last
And make advance the only goal we knew.
The bodies we evolved can't change that quick,
Our brains assume we live by social rules.
We've health, but find new ways of being sick;
The palace that we've built is run by fools.
Our lust for growth's not easy to resist,
But we must start to think, or not exist.

Covid-19

Like fearsome battle colours, breathing masks
Distinguish my assassins from my friends.
While undertakers busy at their tasks,
I wonder now: is this the way it ends?
We're cuckoos in a nest the size of earth
And jostle out all rivals for their space.
With macrofauna gone, we've made a dearth
Of every other beast at startling pace.
What hero from the jungle will come out
To rid the earth of this destructive yob?
Coronavirus steps from its redoubt
In bat's blood; is it equal to the job?
Like Spanish flu and Sars, it's just a test
As nature picks the weapon she likes best.

Kennings

O, great storm bringer, font of hail and rain,
Corruptor of the clouds and of the sky,
Now freed from fossil carbon where you've lain
Since dinosaurs *en masse* lay down to die.
A duvet for the world, its warming pan,
Immersion heater coiled around its girth,
You are the scourge of icebergs, and of man
When coastal plots depreciate in worth.
O, mighty god of thunder, lightning lord,
Who plays with weather as kids treat a toy,
You threaten futures we have not explored
And fates for which we do not have a ploy.
O, climate change, however you are known,
We take the blame; we claim you as our own.

Rubbish

This flipflop had a human owner once,
A woman by the size, but let that be.
We don't know whether genius or dunce;
She let her flipflop flip into the sea.
The ocean has a way to deal with waste,
It bleaches timber, smoothes and frosts our glass,
It has relentless time and shows no haste,
Its work goes on as generations pass.
But now, when human time is near its end,
We start to throw our plastics in the waves.
It's simpler to discard things than to mend,
And buy the new stuff everybody craves.
The ocean's puny – though its breakers crash –
Against our megatons of plastic trash.

Neolithic

The Neolithic was our first mistake,
Though then it seemed to be the perfect plan.
From our adapted life we changed to take
More from the land, then things went down the pan.
Okay, the time it saved was put to use
And art and science flourished in the end,
But power, wealth and status bred abuse
And laws were acted that elites could bend.
Now our new diet's not a boon to health;
We catch new bugs from animals we tame;
With poverty a consequence of wealth,
Nostalgia tints the past from whence we came.
To hunt and gather may be ways we lack;
Our second fault's to dream we can go back.

Last

And there will be a final generation,
The last to click a mouse or swipe a phone,
Who'll have the power to act but not postpone
And not enjoy the prospect of salvation.
When I was young the end we feared was war:
A hostile foe would nuke us as we slept.
Our swift response would be a promise kept
And toxic winds would howl for evermore.
With changing climate, famine's now a threat –
For years the most avoidable of harms.
Our starving future kin with babes in arms
Will surely not forgive us, nor forget.
A message to these remnants now we send:
It was our greed that sped you to your end.

Guns

They say guns don't kill people, people do –
The slogan's cute but not exactly true,
For most policemen, when a shooting's done,
The suspect is a person with a gun.
A sidearm is a sleek and lustrous pet,
A faithful friend, an object of desire;
Extension of your hand, it yearns to fire
A bullet into any likely threat.
A gleaming pistol will accessorise,
Adorning you as no new mobile can.
If you are small, a gun can boost your size;
Just holding it can make you be a man.
Reality beckons; like it or not,
When people have firearms, people get shot.

Online

When chatting with a stranger in a bar,
Who cares if it's high rhetoric or prate?
You're both polite as normal people are,
Despite the heated topics you debate.
For contrast, move the colloquy online,
Where people just like you now congregate.
The atmosphere has now become malign,
The language, civil once, has turned to hate.
Respectful manners help us get along
In social groups that we're adapted for.
In cyberspace, where we do not belong,
We lose our skills at fostering rapport.
Next time you think of typing, 'You're a shite,'
Remember you were born to be polite.

Headcount

Now gather round the table, share the feast;
The cloth is laid, the dishes filled with food;
There's plenty here for dozens more at least –
Bring all your siblings, bring your new-born brood.
Your grandchildren are welcome, take a seat;
And their descendants; let's not count them up.
Sure, if the dining hall becomes replete
We'll pitch a tent outside where we can sup.
But now the kitchen pantry is bereft,
More guests arrive but there's no food for them.
The banquet's done, and though there's nothing left
New guests come in a tide we cannot stem.
This is some party we've had in this hall;
With fewer guests there'd be enough for all.

Tyranny

The untaught infant snatches from his friend,
The criminal thinks rules are his to bend.
We know that crime will never cease to be;
We pay this as the price for feeling free.
We even know that bullies, come the hour,
Can turn to tyrants if they're given power.
With evil men all history is rife
Yet how can they persist in modern life?
Of tyrants in the past we're well aware
(Think Stalin, Hitler, Pol Pot, Kim *grand-père*),
But despots in our century of peace?
(Arise, Erdogan, Putin, Xi, Kim *fils*.)
Concerning bullies, let us covenant
To keep them well away from government.

Religion

The gods have tolled the death knell for ideas,
The doleful bell for independent minds.
Just take a child and fill his head with fears
And watch as his creativeness unwinds.
Imagination dies when clerics speak;
They can't see evolution just needs time.
Their arguments against revealed as weak,
They still deny that life could start in slime.
And when it comes to how we live our lives,
How clear it is how folk should get along,
Religion doesn't trust us and contrives
Divine revenge for every case of wrong.
When gods are given tenure in your head,
Religion strikes imagination dead.

Xenophobia

When stalking on the veldt, it served us well
To know that our companions were like us,
For men to sleep near men without a fuss
And each to help his likeness if he fell.
In time of innocence we kept our place,
We lived with folk who all looked much the same,
Where we could share a language and a name
And, when the water stilled, a kindred face.
What made good sense before now makes no sense;
We dance to music from our former times.
New melodies are needed, novel rhymes
To void the errors of experience.
In sexual ways and race, society
Is made much stronger by variety.

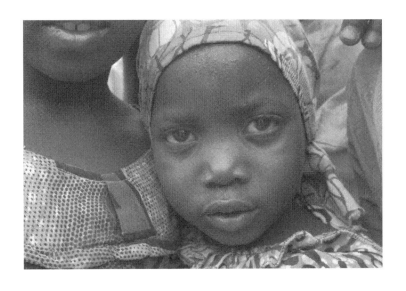

Whale

You used to wade into the shallow sea,
Then deeper, till one day you chose to stay.
Your size surprised you, at your apogee
The deadliest of sharks would turn away.
Millennia of peace came to an end
When tiny land-bound primates tracked you down;
The thickest skin was not enough to fend
Explosive darts or ropes that had you drown.
What memories you must have of cruising free
That drowning, shackled, brings back in a flood,
What hatred as you're winched out of the sea,
The ship that steals you riding in your blood.
We all know well that killing you is wrong;
Hold fast, we'll go, and you can sing your song.

Tyger

The wild ones, do they come to you at night
And do you touch your noses through the wire?
Where you are wronged, do they urge what is right,
And, where you've lost your fight, do they bring fire?
Your feeble keepers tug you by the tail,
And slyly lace the meat they throw to you.
You fight their numbing drugs but always fail,
And pose with tourists when they tell you to.
Your thoughts, of jungle once, are now bereft
Of trodden paths, the earth, the scents you smelt –
They've tranquilised your mind and all they've left:
That proud but empty head and lustrous pelt.
You're prisoner of the profit from the pain
And torment of a tyger on a chain.

Here and now

The landscape shimmers to our music, yet
The earthworm underground, the moth in flight,
The hare that runs, the badger in its sett
Can't hear; their day is quiet as the night.
The power of the cosmos falls in line,
The moon is annexed and the beasts are named.
Though atoms have been split they still combine
And viruses deny that they've been tamed.
The books pile up, the hard drives overload;
As human love's not love to any bird,
The croaking frog's ignored by every toad
And sonnets spill from lofty towers unheard.
The most creative being in creation?
But naturally, by our own estimation.

Capitalism v1.0-3.0

The power firm directors can relax;
Creating profits is simplicity.
The shareholders will spare them from the axe
As long as they make electricity.
Move on, and firms are now responsible,
As others with a stake are borne in mind.
Successful ones must look sustainable;
There's money to be made by seeming kind.
At last the deadly crisis of the earth
Translates in boardrooms to anxiety;
Directors soon will oversee the birth
Of firms that answer to society.
Extinction's threat reluctantly we heed
And find the sin we give up last is greed.

Biodiversity

Now every species generates its kind –
It's what they do, and others do it too.
There isn't space for all, so what we find
Is balances between the types ensue.
But we are wolves of quite a different pack;
We pup just like the others, that's for sure,
But we're so strong there's none can push us back –
We load the scales beyond what they endure.
We cut rainforest trees to raise more beef
And plough up ancient meadows for our grain.
The only living things we grant relief:
The few that can afford our species gain.
A monoculture is abhorred by nature;
That may be how our kind's defined in future.

Disaster movie

The strangers gather at the boarding gate;
Those children play, these adolescents sulk;
Their parents don't foresee their common fate
As outside squats the plane's unlikely bulk.
Those hippies' jeans are not much more than rags;
That woman has a pillow for her neck;
The couple with the Louis Vuitton bags
Have boarding passes for the upper deck.
The nun smiles bravely as she takes her seat.
Is she the only one to feel such fright?
Now calm attendants hand out things to eat;
She's pacified; it's just a routine flight.
Outside, the engines' reassuring whine
Counts out the carbon and the earth's decline.

The end

When our extinction silences the day,
Restoring dark to light-polluted night,
When steel returns to rust and bricks to clay
And tides subside to their accustomed height,
Then there'll be none to keep our sacred list,
Our record of invention and our art,
No tally of achievements will persist,
No evidence of brain, no sign of heart.
Were we as special as we thought we were?
The best there was, the prize of nature's flock?
We took off far too fast, our feet a blur,
And finished in a few ticks of the clock.
Our species had its day, but so did both
The common trilobite and giant sloth.

Notes

An earlier version of *Tyger* appeared in *The Thailand Sonnets*; *Quantum Theory* has been reworked from the original in *Selected Poems*.

Thanks to www.gracies-grannies.com for the postcards of Miss Fernande on page 21. Miss Fernande (1892-1960) was model and lover to Paris-based photographer and postcard publisher Jean Agélou (1878-1921); she also sat for Modigliani.

Thanks to www.phuketwan.com for the photo on page 17.

William Peskett was educated in Belfast, Northern Ireland and at Cambridge University, where he read natural sciences. He has worked in teaching, journalism, marketing, design management and corporate relations. He now lives and writes in Pattaya, Thailand. Peskett has published two volumes of poems, the first of which won an Eric Gregory Award. He has also written novels, short stories, verse, a radio comedy and essays about expat life in his adopted country.

Made in the USA
Monee, IL
26 April 2022

95470311R10042

Also by William Peskett

Fiction: *Pond Life, Losing Yourself, Enhance Your Exports!*

Poetry: *The Nightowl's Dissection, Survivors, Selected Poems*

Verse: *Go-Go Girls, The Thailand Sonnets*

Essays: *If You Can't Stand The Fun, Stay Out Of The Go-Go, Return To The Go-Go*

Short Fiction: *Mango and Sticky Rice, Mist on the Jungle, Sweet Song of the Siren, The Day of the Tiger, Selected Short Stories of Thailand*

Radio: *Deals in Space!*

In Translation: *Riz Gluant à la Mangue, Brume sur la Jungle, Le Chant Ensorcelant de la Sirène, Le Temps des Tigres, Nouvelles Choisies de Thaïlande, Les Sonnets de Thaïlande*

Contact the author, read the blog and find out more on the official website www.williampeskett.com.